JOKES, FUN FACTS & TRICK QUESTIONS

FOR KIDS

BY

ROB HILARIO

TABLE OF CONTENTS

PLEASE LEAVE A REVIEW

Knock-Knock!

I really hope your kids will enjoy this little book. And it would be great if you could take a moment of your time to jot down a short review on the book's Amazon Page. Your feedback is very important to me. It will also help others to make an informed decision before purchasing my book.

THANK YOU!

Rob Hilario

SPORTS & GAMES

Q: **What is a boxer's favorite part of a joke?**

A: The punch-line!

* * *

Q: **What's the difference between a quarterback and a newborn baby?**

A: One takes the snap, the other takes a nap.

* * *

Q: What kind of stories do basketball players tell?

A: Tall Tales.

* * *

Q: Why can't you tell a joke while doing ice skating?

A: Because the ice might crack up!

* * *

Q: What did the archer get when he hit a bullseye?

A: A very angry bull.

* * *

Did you know?

The bullseye is the center of a shooting target. It takes its name from a British coin called "the bull's-eye", which was worth a crown, or five shillings.

* * *

Q: What should you do if you see an elephant playing basketball?

A: Get out of the way!

* * *

Q: Why are spiders good at baseball?

A: Because they know how to catch flies!

* * *

Q: Why was Cinderella such a bad bowler?

A: Her coach was a pumpkin.

* * *

Q: How do we know that soccer referees are happy?

A: Because they whistle at work.

* * *

Q: Why did the soccer ball quit the game?

A: It was tired of being kicked around.

* * *

The term "soccer" originated in England. It's a shortened form of the word "association".

* * *

Q: Why are penguins good race drivers?

A: Because they're always in the pole position!

* * *

Q: What has eighteen legs and catches flies?

A: A baseball team!

* * *

Q: How did the football ground end up in a triangle?

A: Someone took a corner!

* * *

Q: What is the hardest in skydiving?

A: The ground!

* * *

Q: Why should a bowling alley be quiet?

A: So you can hear a pin drop!

* * *

Did you know?

The largest bowling alley in the world is in Japan. It's called "Inazawa Grand Bowling Centre" and it has 116 lanes!

* * *

Q: What do hockey player and magician have in common?

A: They both do hat tricks!

* * *

Q: What did the baseball glove say to the ball?

A: "Catch ya later!"

* * *

Q: What is bug's favorite sport?

A: Cricket!

* * *

Q: How is a baseball team similar to a pancake?

A: They both need a good batter!

* * *

Q: How do you make a fruit punch?

A: Give it boxing lessons.

* * *

Did you know?

The boxing ring is actually a "square". It's called "ring" because in the ancient times a fight between two opponents took place within a drawn circle on the ground.

* * *

Q: What has a spiked tail, plates on its back, and 16 wheels?

A: A dinosaur on roller skates!

* * *

Q: Why did the basketball player go to jail?

A: Because he shot the ball!

* * *

Q: Which baseball player holds water?

A: The pitcher.

* * *

Q: What is a frog's favorite exercise?

A: Jumping Jacks!

* * *

Q: Why do basketball players love cookies?

A: Because they can dunk them.

* * *

Did you know?

"Slam dunk" is a type of basketball shot when a player leaps into the air above the

net's rim and puts the ball straight into the
net.

* * *

Q: What kind of bow cannot be tied?

A: A rainbow!

* * *

Q: Which figure skater can jump higher than the judge's table?

A: Any. A table can't jump.

* * *

Q: Why can't Cinderella play basketball?

A: Because she is always running away from the ball.

* * *

Q: Why can't you play a fair basketball game in the jungle?

A: Too many cheetahs.

* * *

Q: Why can't Tiger Woods listen to music?

A: Because he broke the records.

* * *

Did you know?

Tiger Woods is an American professional golfer and one of the most successful golfers of all time.

Woods has won 18 World Golf Championships.

* * *

Q: What do golf balls and eggs have in common?

A: They're white, they're sold by the dozen, and a week later you have to buy more.

* * *

Q: Why do soccer players do well in school?

A: They know how to use their heads.

* * *

Q: Why didn't the dog want to play football?

A: Because it was a boxer!

* * *

Q: What is harder to catch the faster you run?

A: Your breath.

* * *

Q: Why do figure skaters work in bakeries when they retire?

A: They are great at icing cakes.

* * *

Did you know?

Figure skating was the first winter sport included in the Olympic Games in the 1908 Summer Olympics in London.

* * *

Q: Why can't you play soccer with pigs?

A: They hog the ball.

* * *

Q: Why do some football players never sweat?

A: Because of all the fans!

* * *

Q: Why was the soccer field wet on a sunny day?

A: Because the players dribbled all over it.

* * *

Q: What kind of exercise is best for a swimmer?

A: Pool-ups.

* * *

Did you know?

Elephants are good swimmers. They can swim twenty miles a day using their trunks as natural snorkels!

* * *

Q: Why did the vegetarian stop swimming?

A: She didn't like meets.

* * *

Q: Why did Tarzan spend so much time playing golf?

A: He was perfecting his swing.

TRICK QUESTIONS & RIDDLES (PART 1)

You can see me in water, but I never get wet. What am I?

(Answer: page 68)

* * *

I'm flat when I'm new. I'm fat when you use me. I release my gas when something sharp touches me. What am I?

(Answer: page 69)

* * *

I'm made for one but meant for two; I can be worn for many years but sometimes just a few. You won't ever need me unless you say you do. What am I?

(Answer: page 70)

* * *

I'm tall when I'm young; I'm short when I'm old. What am I?

(Answer: page 71)

* * *

What can point in every direction but can't reach the destination by itself?

(Answer: page 72)

* * *

I am a ship that can be made to ride the greatest waves. I am not built by tools but built by hearts and minds. What am I?

(Answer: page 73)

* * *

The more you have of it, the less you see. What is it?

(Answer: page 74)

* * *

You answer me, but I never ask you a question.
What am I?

(Answer: page 75)

NATURE & GEOGRAPHY

Q: What washes up on small beaches?

A: Microwaves!

* * *

Q: What did the big flower say to the small flower?

A: "What's up, bud?"

* * *

Q: Teacher: What can you tell us about the Dead Sea?

A: Student: I didn't even know it was sick!

* * *

Q: What kind of flowers grow on your face?

A: Tulips!

* * *

Q: Why did the map always get in trouble?

A: It had bad latitude.

* * *

Did you know?

Latitudes are horizontal lines on the globe. They are also known as parallels as they are at an equal distance from each other and they never meet.

* * *

Q: How do trees get on the internet?

A: They log in.

* * *

Q: What kind of tree you can place in your hand?

A: A palm tree!

* * *

Q: When is the moon the heaviest?

A: When it's full!

* * *

Q: What did the beaver say to the tree?

A: It's been nice gnawing you!

* * *

Q: What did Mars say to Saturn?

A: Give me a ring sometime.

* * *

Did you know?

Saturn is the second biggest planet, but it's also the lightest one. It is surrounded by a system of rings that stretches out into space for thousands of miles.

* * *

Q: What is the biggest mark in the world?

A: Denmark.

* * *

Q: What did the tornado say to a car?

A: Want to go for a spin!

* * *

Q: What is the biggest cow in the world that doesn't give any milk?

A: MosCOW.

* * *

Q: What kind of songs do the planets sing?

A: Nep-tunes!

* * *

Q: Which member of the orchestra is most likely to get hit by lightning?

A: The conductor.

* * *

Did you know?

A conductor is a material which electricity, heat or sound can flow through.

* * *

Q: What did the small tree say to the big tree?

A: Leaf me alone!

* * *

Q: How can you tell that compasses and scales are intelligent?

A: Because they all graduated.

* * *

Q: What is the biggest pan in the world?

A: JaPAN!

* * *

Q: Why don't you see penguins in Great Britain?

A: Because they're afraid of Wales.

* * *

Q: What did the ground say to the earthquake?

A: "You crack me up!"

* * *

Q: If you put a green rock in the Red Sea, what will happen?

A: It will get wet!

* * *

Did you know?

The Red Sea is an inlet of the Indian Ocean between Africa and Asia. Most of the time, the Red Sea is a bright bluish-green color, but sometimes it becomes reddish-brown due to a water plant called "cyanobacteria algae."

* * *

Q: What do maps and fish have in common?

A: They have scales.

* * *

Q: What did the cloud say to the lightning bolt?

A: You are shocking!

* * *

Q: Which country is the fastest?

A: Rush-a!

* * *

Q: What is the happiest state in the USA?

A: Merry-land!

* * *

Q: Why do Chinese men eat more rice than Japanese men?

A: There are more Chinese men than Japanese men!

* * *

Did you know?

China has the largest population in the world, with over 1.38 billion people.

The population of Japan is over 127 million people.

* * *

Q: Who was Mississippi married too?

A: Mister Sippi!

* * *

Q: What is the opposite of a cold front?

A: A warm back!

* * *

Q: What is a tornado's favorite game?

A: Twister!

* * *

A: What is the difference between a horse and the weather?

Q: One is reined up and the other rains down!

* * *

Q: What type of lightning likes to play soccer?

A: Ball lightning!

* * *

Did you know?

Ball lightning is a very rare form of lightning. It usually appears in a thunderstorm as a reddish, luminous ball that floats through the air.

* * *

Q: How did Christopher Columbus pay for his trip to the new land?

A: He used his Discover card.

* * *

Q: Why did the archaeologist put a band-aid on the map?

A: Because it had a bleeding edge.

* * *

Q: What do you call a beautiful volcano?

A: Lava-ble!

* * *

Q: What did the small rock say to the big muscle rock?

A: I wish I were boulder!

* * *

Q: Why do people wear shamrocks on St. Patrick's Day?

A: Real rocks are very heavy!

* * *

Did you know?

The name shamrock is derived from Irish word "seamróg", which means "little clover" or "young clover".

* * *

Q: **What kind of pudding roams in the Arctic Circle?**

A: Moose.

* * *

Q: **What do you call the city without any small apples?**

A: Mini-apple-less.

* * *

Q: **What is smarter, latitude or longitude?**

A: Longitude, because it has 360 degrees.

* * *

Q: **Which rock band has four men that don't sing?**

A: Mount Rushmore!

* * *

Did you know?

Mount Rushmore National Memorial is a sculpture of four American Presidents: George Washington, Thomas Jefferson, Theodore Roosevelt, and Abraham Lincoln, carved into the side of Mount Rushmore in the Black Hills of South Dakota, USA.

* * *

Q: Did you hear about Italy?

A: It got Hungary, ate Turkey, went shopping in Iceland, slipped on Greece, and then got eaten by Wales.

* * *

Q: What did one pyramid say to the other?

A: How's your mummy doing?

* * *

Q: Where is the English Channel?

A: It depends on who is your cable provider.

* * *

Did you know?

The English Channel is a body of water that separates the island of Great Britain from the rest of Europe.

In French, it is called La Manche ("the sleeve")

TRICK QUESTIONS & RIDDLES (PART 2)

I am a box that holds keys without locks, yet they can unlock your soul. What am I?

(Answer: page 76)

* * *

What is as big as you are and yet does not weigh anything?

(Answer: page 77)

* * *

I have an eye but am blind; a sea, but no water; a bee, but no honey; tea but no coffee; and a why, but no answer. What am I?

(Answer: page 78)

You go at red but stop at green. What am I?

(Answer: page 79)

* * *

What can split itself before splitting something else?

(Answer: page 80)

* * *

I jump when I walk and sit when I stand. What am I?

(Answer: page 81)

* * *

A box without hinges, lock or key, yet golden treasure lies within. What is it?

(Answer: page 82)

* * *

What goes thousands of miles but never moves?

(Answer: page 83)

FOOD & SNACKS

Q: **What kind of table you can eat?**

A: VegeTABLE.

* * *

Q: **Why did the donut go to the dentist?**

A: He needed a chocolate filling.

* * *

Q: **What do polar bears eat for dinner?**

A: ICE BERG-ers!

* * *

Q: **What do you call a monkey with a banana in each ear?**

A: You can call it whatever you want, it can't hear you!

* * *

Q: **What does a nut say when it sneezes?**

A: Cashew!

* * *

Did you know?

Unlike other nuts the cashew does not grow inside of the fruit, but instead on the outside of it, hanging from the base of a crab apple, called a "cashew apple."

* * *

Q: What did the mamma tomato say to the little baby tomato?

A: Catch up!

* * *

Q: What's in an astronaut's favorite meal?

A: Launch meat.

* * *

Q: Why was the boy staring at the can of orange juice?

A: Because it said "concentrate".

* * *

Q: Why shouldn't you tell secrets on a farm?

A: Because the potatoes have eyes, the corn has ears, and the beans stalk.

* * *

Q: Why was the cucumber mad?

A: Because it was in a pickle!

* * *

Did you know?

To be "in a pickle" means to be in a difficult, troublesome situation.

* * *

Q: What did the farmer give his wife for Valentine's Day?

A: Corn Rows.

* * *

Q: What is Fast Food?

A: A chicken running down the road.

* * *

Q: How do you call a fake noodle?

A: An ImPasta!

* * *

Q: Why did the grape stop running down the road?

A: Because he ran out of juice.

* * *

Q: **What kind of cheese is made backwards?**

A: Edam!

* * *

Did you know?

Edam is a type cheese that originated in the Netherlands. It is named after the town of Edam in the province of North Holland.

* * *

Q: **What did one plate say to another?**

A: Lunch is on me!

* * *

Q. **If you divide an orange between five friends, what do they each get?**

A. Sticky fingers.

* * *

Q: **What food is good for your brain?**

A: Noodle soup!

* * *

Q: Where do burgers go dancing?

A: To a meat ball!

* * *

Q: What is the most mysterious vegetable?

A: The uniCORN.

* * *

Q: What do you call a dog with a high fever?

A: A hot dog.

* * *

Did you know?

The term "hot-dog" came from a belief that sausage makers used actual dog meat. In many places, hot dogs are also called red-hots.

* * *

Q: What candy is for girls only?

A: HER-SHEy's Kisses.

* * *

Q: **Why was the blueberry sad?**

A: Because her mom was in a jam!

* * *

Q: **What do you give to a sick lemon?**

A: Lemon aid!

* * *

Q: **Why did the tomato turn red?**

A: Because it saw the salad dressing!

* * *

Q: **What kind of apple is not an apple?**

A: A pineapple!

* * *

Did you know?

Pineapples take about 18-20 months to become ready to harvest. One pineapple plant can produce only one pineapple fruit at a time.

* * *

Q: **Why did the cookie go to the doctor?**

A: Because it was feeling crummy!

* * *

Q: **What did the astronaut say when he stepped on a chocolate bar?**

A: I set foot on Mars!

* * *

Q: **Why did the man climb on the roof of the restaurant?**

A: Because the manager told him the meal was on the house.

* * *

Q: **What is it called when you put a cow in an elevator?**

A: Raising the steaks.

* * *

Q: **Why was the potato such a bully?**

A: Because it wasn't a sweet potato.

* * *

Did you know?

Under favorable conditions, sweet potatoes can be stored for up to 10 months without spoiling.

* * *

Q: Why do potatoes make such good detectives?

A: Because they keep their eyes peeled.

* * *

Q: Waiter, will my pizza be long?

A: No, it will be round!

* * *

Q: Why did the baker stop making doughnuts?

A: Because she was bored with the hole business!

* * *

Q: **What kind of shoes do you make from bananas?**

A: A slippers!

* * *

Q: **What did the pepperoni say to the cook?**

A: Do you wanna pizza me?!

* * *

Did you know?

The word "pizza" dates back over a thousand years. It was first documented in the Italian city of Gaeta in 997 AD.

* * *

Q: **Why did the French fry win the race?**

A: Because it was fast food!

* * *

Q: **How can you fix a broken tomato?**

A: With tomato paste!

* * *

Q: **What do you call a bear with no teeth?**

A: A gummy bear!

* * *

Q: **Do you want to hear a joke about pizza?**

A: Never mind, it's too cheesy.

* * *

Q: **What is Dracula's favorite fruit?**

A: Neck-tarines.

* * *

Q: **What do you get when you mix lemons with gunpowder?**

A: Lemonades.

* * *

Did you know?

Lemonade can trace its origins to the ancient Egypt where lemon juice was mixed with sugar to make a beverage known as "qatarmizat". The "ade" in lemonade means that the product is not 100% juice.

* * *

Q: What day do potatoes hate?

A: Fry-day!

* * *

Q: What do you get when you cross a computer with a hamburger?

A: A big MAC!

* * *

Q. What's a zombie's favorite soup?

A. Scream of tomato.

* * *

Q: Why did the student eat his homework?

A: The teacher told him it was a piece of cake.

* * *

Q: How do lemons ask for a hug?

A: "Give us a squeeze!"

* * *

Q: What's the worst thing about being an octopus?

A: Washing your hands before breakfast.

* * *

Q: What do zombies eat on Halloween?

A: Ghoulash!

* * *

Did you know?

Goulash is a stew of meat and vegetables, seasoned with paprika and other spices. It is popular in Central Europe.

* * *

Q: Why doesn't anyone laugh at the gardener's jokes?

A: Because they are too CORNey.

TRiCK QUESTiONS & RiDDLES (PART 3)

What stays in the corner, but travels around the world?

(Answer: page 84)

* * *

What is black and white and read all over?

(Answer: page 85)

* * *

I can be long, I can be short. I can be grown, I can be bought. I can be painted or left bare. I can be round, or even square. What am I?

(Answer: page 86)

* * *

What body part is pronounced as one letter but written with three. Only two different letters are used?

(Answer: page 87)

* * *

At night they come without being fetched, and by day they are lost without being stolen. What are they?

(Answer: page 88)

* * *

What do you throw out when you want to use it, but take in when you don't want to use it?

(Answer: page 89)

* * *

Give me food, and I will live. Give me water, and I will die. What am I?

(Answer: page 90)

* * *

Large as a mountain, small as a pea, endlessly swimming in a waterless sea.

(Answer: page 91)

* * *

What tastes better than it smells?

(Answer: page 92)

LITTLE OF EVERYTHING

Q: Why did the man run around the bed?

A: He wanted to catch up on his sleep!

* * *

Q: Why did the boy bury his flashlight?

A: Because the batteries were dead.

* * *

Q: Why did the invisible man quit the job?

A: He couldn't see himself doing it.

* * *

Q: What kind of driver needs no license?

A: Screwdriver!

* * *

Q: What is a kangaroo's favorite year?

A: A leap year.

* * *

Did you know?

Leap Year is a year with one extra day – February 29. It has 366 days instead of 365 and occurs every 4 years.

* * *

Q: Why do bicycles fall over?

A: Because they are two-tired!

* * *

Q: What has four wheels and flies?

A: A garbage truck!

* * *

Q: What kind of music is balloon scared of?

A: Pop music!

* * *

Q: What is the most dangerous job in Transylvania?

A: Dracula's dentist.

* * *

Q: What is yellow, big and comes every morning to brighten mom's day?

A: School Bus.

* * *

Did you know?

The word "bus" comes from the Latin word "omnibus", which means "for all." Buses were the first form of public transport.

* * *

Q: What has four legs but can't walk?

A: A table!

* * *

Q: What do you call a pig that knows kung-fu?

A: A Pork Chop.

* * *

Q: What nails does carpenter hate to hit?

A: Fingernails!

* * *

Q: What animal is always lost?

A: A where wolf.

* * *

Q: Why did the skeleton go to the piano store?

A: To buy organs!

* * *

Did you know?

The pipe organ is the earliest keyboard instrument.

* * *

Q: Which question can no one answer with a "yes"?

A: "Are you sleeping?"

* * *

Q: What do you call a fly without wings?

A: A walk!

* * *

Q: What has forty feet and can sing?

A: The school choir!

* * *

Q: What's the difference between a newspaper and a TV?

A: Have you ever tried swatting a fly with a TV?

* * *

Q: Why did Mickey Mouse go into space?

A: He wanted to find Pluto!

* * *

Did you know?

Pluto is the smallest and furthest planet from the Sun in our solar system. It is named after the Roman god of the underworld, and officially classified as a dwarf planet.

* * *

Q: Which word is spelled incorrectly in the dictionary?

A: Incorrectly!

* * *

Q: What do you call someone with no body and no nose?

A: Nobody knows!

* * *

Q: What kind of shoes do spies wear?

A: Sneakers.

* * *

Q: What time is it when a hippo sits on your fence?

A: Time to buy a new fence.

* * *

Q: How can you make seven an even number?

A: Take the "s" out!

* * *

Did you know?

An even number is an integer that can be evenly divided by two.

* * *

Q: What room is useless for zombies?

A: A living room!

* * *

Q: Why can't you play hide-and-seek with mountains?

A: Because they're always peaking.

* * *

Q: Why did Tigger stick his head in the toilet?

A: Because he was looking for Pooh!

* * *

Q: What do, Christopher Columbus, George Washington and Abraham Lincoln all have in common?

A: They were all born on holidays!

* * *

Q: What is the longest word?

A: Smiles, because there is a mile between two S's.

* * *

Did you know?

The longest non-coined word in the English language is "Antidisestablishmentarianism".

* * *

Q: Why was the broom late?

A: It over swept!

* * *

Q: How do you know if there's a dinosaur hiding under your bed?

A: Your nose hits the ceiling!

* * *

Q: Why don't cars play football?

A: Because they only have one boot.

* * *

Q: What's the biggest mouse in the world?

A: HippopotaMOUSE.

* * *

Q: What's black and white and makes a loud noise?

A: A zebra with a drum kit.

* * *

Did you know?

Every zebra has a unique pattern of black and white stripes.

* * *

Q: What color can you eat?

A: Orange!

* * *

Q: What do frogs order in the restaurant?

A: French Flies.

* * *

Q: What's the hottest part of a room?

A: The corner, it is 90 degrees.

* * *

Q: Why do we put candles on top of a birthday cake?

A: Because it's too hard to put them on the bottom!

* * *

Q: Why did the computer go to the dentist?

A: Because it had Bluetooth.

* * *

Did you know?

The word "Bluetooth" comes from the name of the tenth-century king Harald Blatand (Bluetooth) of Denmark who united warring tribes into a single kingdom.

* * *

Q: Why is Peter Pan always flying?

A: He neverlands!

* * *

Q: What do you call a funny mountain?

A: Hill-arious!

* * *

Q: What did the triangle say to the circle?

A: You are so pointless.

* * *

Q: Why was the laptop cold?

A: It left its Windows open!

* * *

Q: What did the traffic lights say to the car?

A: Don't look now. I'm changing!

* * *

Did you know?

The first electric traffic signal was installed more than 100 years ago in Cleveland, Ohio on August 5, 1914.

* * *

Q: Why did the smartphone need glasses?

A: Because it lost all of its contacts.

* * *

Q: What do you call security guards in a Samsung store?

A: Guardians of the Galaxy.

* * *

Q: Why did the barber win the race?

A: Because he knew a shortcut.

* * *

Did you know?

The word barber comes from the Latin word "barba", meaning beard. Barbering is one of the oldest professions in the world.

TRICK QUESTIONS & RIDDLES (PART 4)

You hear it speak, for it has a hard tongue. But it cannot breathe, for it has not a lung. What is it?

(Answer: page 93)

* * *

You can hold me in your hand and yet I can fill the entire room. What am I?

(Answer: page 94)

* * *

What turns everything around but does not move?

(Answer: page 95)

* * *

What has 10 letters and starts with gas?

(Answer: page 96)

* * *

I have two backbones and thousands of ribs and I stretch across the land. What am I?

(Answer: page 97)

* * *

I have six faces but not even one body connected. 21 eyes in total but cannot see. What am I?

(Answer: page 98)

* * *

Take off my skin - I won't cry, but you will! What am I?

(Answer: page 99)

* * *

What always goes to bed with its shoes on?

(Answer: page 100)

* * *

No matter how much rain comes down, it won't get any wetter. What is it?

(Answer: page 101)

OTHER WORKS:

"HILARIO'S BOOKS FOR KIDS VOL. 1"

YOUR REVIEW

Knock-Knock!

I hope your kids have enjoyed reading this little book. And it would be great if you could take a moment of your time to jot down a short review on the book's Amazon Page. Your feedback is very important to me. It will also help others to make an informed decision before purchasing my book.

THANK YOU!

Rob Hilario

REFLECTION

BALOON

WEDDING RING

CANDLE

YOUR FINGER

FRIENDSHIP

DARKNESS

PHONE

PIANO

SHADOW

ALPHABET

WATERMELLON

LiGHTNiNG

KANGAROO

EGG

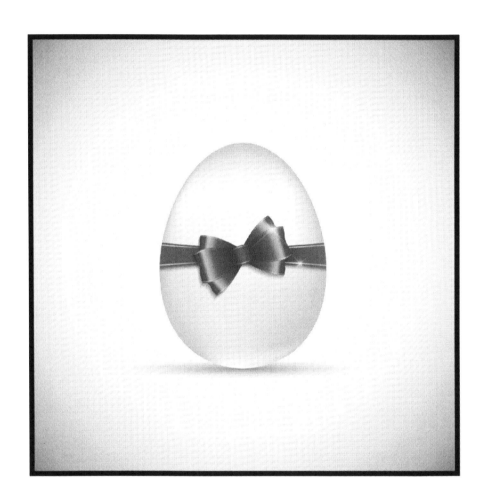

HiGHWAY

STAMP

NEWSPAPER

FINGERNAIL

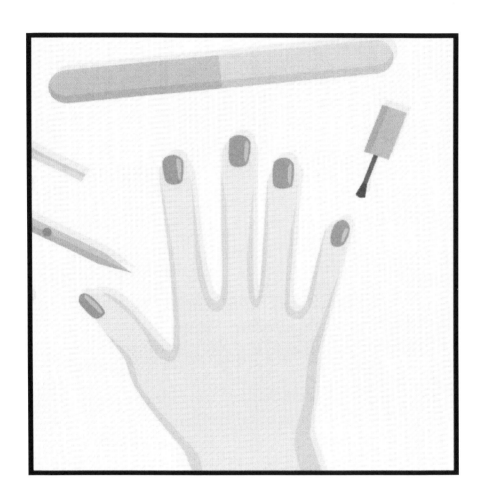

EYE

STARS

ANCHOR

FiRE

ASTEROID

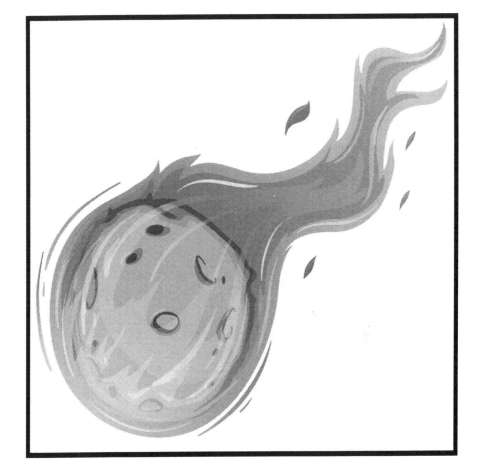

TONGUE

BELL

LIGHT BULB

MiRROR

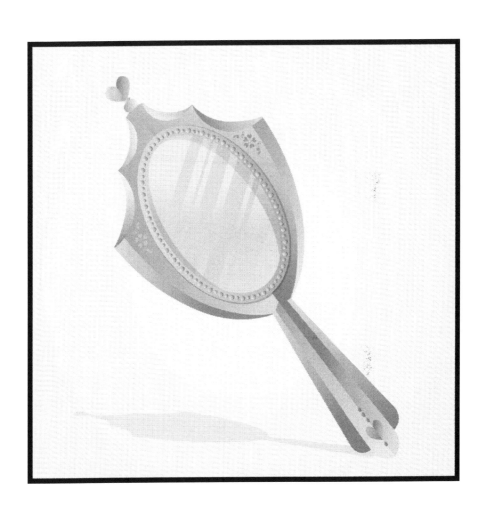

AUTOMOBILE

TRAIN TRACKS

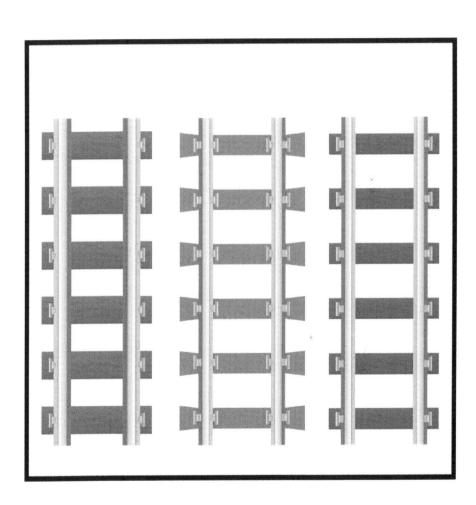

DICE

ONION

HORSE

WATER

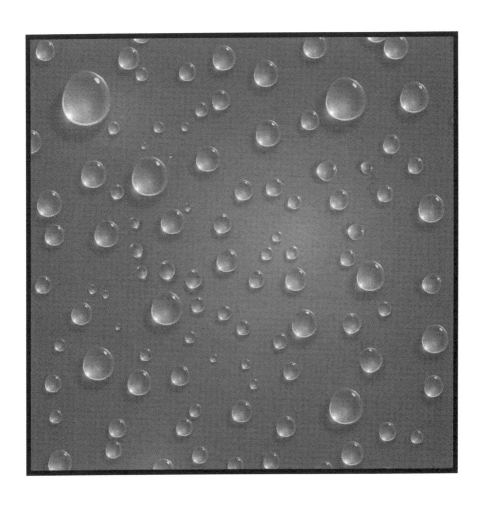

CREDITS

All images designed by: brgfx / Freepik, macrovector / Freepik, iconicbestiary / Freepik, Dooder / Freepik, Frimufilms / Freepik, iconicbestiary / Freepik, Johndory / Freepik, macrovector / Freepik, Articular / Freepik, Ajipebriana / Freepik, Kjpargeter / Freepik, Alekksall / Freepik.

24925613R00057

Made in the USA
Lexington, KY
18 December 2018